KOYOHARU GOTOUGE

They're publishing a graphic novel by me! Thank you! And heartfelt thanks to all the readers, my editors over the years, my assistants, everyone in the *Jump* editorial department, everyone at the printer, the people who designed the book, and the many other people who have offered their help!

DEMON SLAYER:
KIMETSU NO YAIBA
VOLUME 1
Shonen Jump Edition

Story and Art by
KOYOHARU GOTOUGE

KIMETSU NO YAIBA
© 2016 by Koyoharu Gotouge
All rights reserved. First published in Japan in 2016 by SHUEISHA Inc., Tokyo. English translation rights arranged by SHUEISHA Inc.

TRANSLATION John Werry
ENGLISH ADAPTATION Stan!
TOUCH-UP ART & LETTERING John Hunt
DESIGN Adam Grano
EDITOR Mike Montesa

The stories, characters and incidents mentioned in this publication are entirely fictional.

No portion of this book may be reproduced or transmitted in any form or by any means without written permission from the copyright holders.

Printed in Canada

Published by VIZ Media, LLC
P.O. Box 77010
San Francisco, CA 94107

10 9 8 7
First printing, July 2018
Seventh printing, March 2021

PARENTAL ADVISORY
DEMON SLAYER: KIMETSU NO YAIBA is rated T for Teen and recommended for ages 13 and up. This volume contains realistic and fantasy violence.

viz.com

1
CRUELTY
DEMON SLAYER
KIMETSU NO YAIBA
KOYOHARU GOTOUGE

CONTENTS

Chapter 1
CRUELTY
5

Chapter 2
THE STRANGER
61

Chapter 3
TO RETURN BY DAWN WITHOUT FAIL
87

Chapter 4
TANJIRO'S JOURNAL, PART 1
111

Chapter 5
TANJIRO'S JOURNAL, PART 2
131

Chapter 6
A MOUNTAIN OF HANDS
151

Chapter 7
SPIRITS OF THE DECEASED
171

DEMON SLAYER
KIMETSU NO YAIBA

1

CRUELTY

HOW DID THIS HAPPEN?
CHAPTER 1: CRUELTY
YOUR BIG BROTHER IS DEFINITELY GOING TO SAVE YOU!
NEZUKO ...
DON'T DIE.
DON'T DIE.
YOU CAN'T DIE.
I'M GONNA SAVE YOU.

CHAPTER 1: CRUELTY

DEMON
SLAYER
KIMETSU NO YAIBA

TANJIRO!

YOU DON'T HAVE TO GO.
IT'S SNOWING AND IT'S DANGER-OUS.

YOUR FACE IS PITCH-BLACK.
COME HERE.

THANK YOU.

I WANT US TO HAVE A GREAT NEW YEAR'S FEAST, SO I'LL GO SELL AS MUCH CHARCOAL AS I CAN...
...EVEN IF IT'S JUST A LITTLE.

WHAAAAA?!
I WANNA GO TOO!
TANJIRO, ARE YOU GOING TO TOWN AGAIN TODAY?

...SO HE CAN'T PULL YOU WHEN YOU'RE TIRED.
HE ISN'T TAKING THE CART TODAY...

BUT MOM!
NO. YOU CAN'T WALK FAST LIKE TANJIRO.
NO.

I WILL, BUT...
...I WAS HOPING WE'D DO IT TOGETHER.

I wanna go with you!
TAKEO ...
I KNOW YOU CAN'T DO A LOT, BUT CUT A LITTLE WOOD TODAY. OKAY?

HURRY BACK, OKAY?
BE CARE-FUL!
NEZUKO ...
I WAS PUTTING ROKUTA TO SLEEP...
...BUT I HEARD ALL THE COMMO-TION.
TANJIRO!
SEE YOU LATER!
...SO THEY'VE STARTED CLINGING TO YOU.
THEY'VE BEEN SO LONELY SINCE FATHER DIED...

IT'S ALWAYS CHANGING.
BUT LIFE IS LIKE THE WEATHER ...
...AND THE SNOW WON'T ALWAYS KEEP FALLING.
IT WON'T ALWAYS BE EASY...
...THE SMELL OF BLOOD IN THE AIR.
WHEN HAPPINESS ENDS THERE'S ALWAYS...
OUR LIFE ISN'T EASY, BUT WE'RE HAPPY.
OH, TANJIRO!

THANKS FOR FIXING MY SHOJI DOOR THE OTHER DAY!
YOU'LL CATCH A COLD!
YOU CAME DOWN THE MOUNTAIN ON A DAY LIKE TODAY? YOU WORK SO HARD!
GIVE ME SOME CHARCOAL TOO!
HEY! SELL ME SOME CHAR-COAL!

HELP ME!
SHE SAYS I BROKE A DISH!
SMELL IT!

YOU'RE JUST IN TIME!
AAAH! TANJIRO!

SNIFF

SNIFF
SNIFF

WILL YOU HELP ME CARRY SOME BUNDLES?!
TANJIRO!
I TOLD YOU IT WASN'T ME!

A CAT? OH DEAR.
I SMELL A CAT.
SEEEE ?!

WHEW! IT'S GETTING LATE!
TP TP TP

IT'S TOO DANGER-OUS!

HEY, TAN-JIRO! YOU AREN'T...
...GOING BACK UP THE MOUNTAIN ARE YOU?!

BUT...
IT'S ALL RIGHT. YOU'RE WELCOME HERE.
YOU CAN STAY HERE.
PLEASE.
COME BACK.
I'VE GOT A GOOD NOSE FOR TROUBLE. I'LL BE FINE.
YOU DON'T WANT TO RUN INTO ANY DEMONS.
SO YOU SHOULDN'T WALK AROUND AT NIGHT.
EAT, THEN SLEEP. YOU CAN GET UP AND GO HOME EARLY TOMORROW.
FOR AGES...
... MAN-EATING DEMONS HAVE ROAMED THESE WOODS AFTER DARK.

THERE'S NO NEED TO FEAR. THERE'S NO SUCH THING AS DEMONS.

NEXT TIME, I'LL BRING MY LITTLE BROTHERS.

OLD MAN SABURO LIVES ALONE BECAUSE HE LOST HIS FAMILY. HE MUST BE LONELY.

BUT NOW THAT I THINK OF IT...

...MY GRANDMOTHER SAID THE SAME THING BEFORE SHE DIED.
WHEN HAPPI-NESS ENDS THERE'S ALWAYS...
...THE SMELL OF BLOOD IN THE AIR.
HFF
HFF

WHAT HAP—
WHAT HAPPENED ?!
AGH!
WHAT THE...?

NEZUKO ...
ROKUTA ...

TAKEO...
SHIGERU ...

MOTHER ...
HANAKO ...

MAYBE A DOCTOR CAN SAVE HER.
ONLY NEZUKO'S BODY WAS STILL WARM.
MAYBE A BEAR TOO HUNGRY TO HIBERNATE?
HOW DID THIS HAPPEN? A BEAR?

KEEP GOING!
MOVE YOUR FEET FASTER.
THE AIR'S SO COLD IT'S FREEZING MY LUNGS.
SO HARD TO BREATHE!
I HAVE TO SAVE YOU.
TWITCH
I WON'T LET YOU DIE.
IT'S STILL A LONG WAY TO TOWN.
YOUR BIG BROTHER WILL SAVE YOU!

AAAAH!
GRRAA
SHWF
?!
WHMP
I'M SLIP—
OH NO!

FWUNG!
BUT IT ALSO MADE ME SLIP!
THE SNOW...
...SAVED ME.
SHWF
NEZUKO!
!!

YOU SHOULDN'T BE UP!
LET ME...
...CARRY YOU INTO TOWN!

NEZUKO!
ARE YOU ALL RIGHT?
SHF

NEZUKO ...

WHMPH
OMP
CH
I THOUGHT OF WHAT OLD MAN SABURO SAID.
A DEMON!
WAS NEZUKO ...
...A MAN-EATING DEMON?
NO, THAT WAS IM-POSSIBLE.
NEZUKO HAS BEEN HUMAN...
...SINCE THE DAY SHE WAS BORN.

...FALLEN OVER ROKUTA, LIKE SHE WAS PROTECTING HIM.
BUT NEZUKO COULDN'T HAVE DONE ALL THAT. I FOUND HER...
BUT THIS NEZUKO ...
...SMELLS OF BLOOD AND DEATH.
WHOOMP
SHE DIDN'T HAVE ANY BLOOD ON HER MOUTH OR HANDS.
AND THERE'S YET...
SKRRR
SHFF
SKRK
...ANOTHER SMELL...

WHAT-EVER THE REASON ...
...SHE'S GROWING BIGGER...
KRK
...AND SHE'S GETTING STRON-GER!
KRK
WHILE I WAS SAFELY ASLEEP IN TOWN, SOMETHING HORRIBLE...
...HAPPENED TO MY WHOLE FAMILY.
HOW THEY MUST HAVE SUFFERED.
...AND I WASN'T THERE TO HELP THEM.
KRK
I HAVE TO SAVE NEZUKO IF I CAN!
KRK
BUT SHE'S SO STRONG! I CAN'T PUSH HER AWAY!
NEZUKO!

BE STRONG!
YOU CAN DO IT!
DON'T TURN INTO A DEMON!

HOLD ON, NEZUKO!
FIGHT IT! FIGHT FOR YOUR LIFE!

PLIP
PLIP
PLIP

NEZUKO!

!!
GRAB

FWSH
SNAP

WHO...

FMP

WHO IS THAT?

*AKKIMESSATSU, DESTROYER OF DEMONS
A KATANA...
WHY DO YOU PROTECT HER?

GRAAAR
S-SISTER...
SHE'S MY...
...LITTLE SISTER!

THAT IS YOUR LITTLE SISTER?

GRAAH
RAAGH

SLATCH

DASH

...

GRAAAH!
NEZUKO!

HW
SH
!

DON'T MOVE.

WAIT! NEZUKO HASN'T KILLED ANYONE!

SO OF COURSE, I'LL TAKE YOUR LITTLE SISTER'S HEAD TOO.
KILLING DEMONS IS MY JOB.

THAT MUST BE WHO KILLED EVERYONE!
...FROM SOMEONE I'VE NEVER SMELLED BEFORE!
THERE WAS A SCENT AT MY HOUSE...

THAT'S EASY. DEMON BLOOD GOT IN HER WOUND, SO SHE'S TRANSFORMED INTO A DEMON.
GRAAR!
NOT NEZUKO!
I DON'T KNOW WHAT'S MAKING HER ACT LIKE THIS...
BUT...

THAT IS HOW MAN-EATING DEMONS MULTIPLY.

NO! I'M SURE SHE KNOWS WHO I AM!
A MOMENT AGO SHE ALMOST ATE *YOU!*
NEZUKO WOULD NEVER EAT ANYONE!

I'LL FIND A WAY TO CURE HER!
I'LL MAKE HER HUMAN AGAIN!
I WON'T LET HER HURT ANYONE!

I'LL FIND A WAY! I SWEAR! PLEASE DON'T KILL HER!

A HUMAN WHO BECOMES A DEMON CANNOT GO BACK.
SHE WON'T GET BETTER.

SHNNG
...SO...

I'LL ALSO FIND THE ONE THAT KILLED MY FAMILY!
I'LL DO ALL THAT, SO...
...SO...

I CAN'T LOSE NEZUKO TOO!
STOP!
PLEASE, STOP.
PLEASE...
PLEASE DON'T KILL MY LITTLE SISTER!
PLEASE...

NEVER LEAVE YOURSELF SO DEFENSELESS IN FRONT OF AN ENEMY!

STOP BOWING SO PITIFULLY!
IF THAT WORKED, YOUR FAMILY WOULD STILL BE ALIVE!

FLINCH

...CURE HIS LITTLE SISTER?
OR EVEN *FIND* HIS ENEMY?
HOW CAN A WEAKLING LIKE YOU, WHO BOWS DOWN WHEN IT'S TIME TO FIGHT, TO KILL OR BE KILLED... HOW CAN SUCH A MAN...

...YOU MUST FIGHT FOR IT!
IF YOU WANT SOME-THING...

DEMONS MIGHT KNOW HOW TO CURE YOUR LITTLE SISTER...
...NO DEMON WILL RESPECT YOUR WHINING AND BEGGING!
... BUT ...

THE MEEK HAVE NO POWER AND NO OPTIONS!
THE STRONG WILL CRUSH THEM IN EVERY WAY!

BEFORE ...
WHY DID YOU COVER YOUR SISTER?
DID YOU THINK THAT WOULD PROTECT HER?!

AND FOR THAT MATTER, I DON'T RESPECT YOU EITHER!
THAT'S REALITY!

THAT'S HOW I WAS ABLE TO TAKE HER!
WHY DIDN'T YOU THROW YOUR HATCHET?
WHY DID YOU SHOW ME YOUR BACK?!

HFF
HFF
HFF

GRAAH!
I SHOULD HAVE SKEWERED YOU BOTH!
THUD

YOUR HEART IS CRUSHED.
YOUR FAMILY IS DEAD AND YOUR SISTER HAS BECOME A DEMON.
I KNOW YOUR PAIN, HOW YOU MUST WANT TO CRY OUT.
DON'T CRY.
DON'T DESPAIR.
THOSE THINGS WILL DO YOU NO GOOD.
BUT THERE IS NO TURNING BACK TIME.
...YOUR FAMILY MIGHT HAVE SURVIVED.
IF I'D COME HALF A DAY SOONER ...
ANGER THAT BECOMES THE UNWAVERING FORCE THAT DRIVES YOUR LIMBS.
...THAT GIVES NO QUARTER.
STRONG, PURE ANGER...
FILL YOUR HEART WITH ANGER.

AND THEY CERTAINLY CANNOT AVENGE YOUR FAMILY.
...CANNOT PROTECT YOUR SISTER OR FIND HER A CURE.
WEAKNESS AND EMPTY PROMISES ...

W...

SHANK

GNGH
NOOO!
FWIP

KTAK
WHA

AAAAH!
WHOK

WHAT A FOOL!
A SIMPLE, HEAD-ON ATTACK RELYING ON PURE EMOTION.

ナイ
OK
滅殺

BUMP
WHERE IS HIS HATCHET?
WHISH

FWIP
FWIP

THOK
JUST BEFORE PASSING BEHIND THE TREE, HE THREW A ROCK...
...AND WHILE HIDDEN BY THE TREE HE THREW HIS HATCHET.

...WAS TO STRIKE ME DOWN AFTER I KILLED HIM.
HE KNEW HE COULDN'T WIN AGAINST ME, SO HIS PLAN...
HE HID HIS HAND SO I WOULDN'T SEE HE WAS UNARMED.
GRAAR!
THIS KID...
WHOK

NO! I'M TOO LATE!
SKF
SHE'S ABOUT TO EAT HIM!
NEZUKO...

NEZUKO WOULD NEVER EAT ANYONE!
NOT NEZUKO!

HE WOULDN'T BE...

...THE FIRST TO SAY THAT AND THEN GET EATEN ANYWAY.

STARVING DEMONS WILL KILL AND EAT THEIR OWN PARENTS AND SIBLINGS.
BECAUSE THEY NEED THE ENERGY.
I'VE SEEN IT COUNT-LESS TIMES.
...NOT TO MENTION THE STRENGTH IT TOOK TO TRANSFORM INTO A DEMON. SHE MUST BE DOUBLY STARVED RIGHT NOW...
...AND MUST WANT TO EAT HUMAN FLESH AS SOON AS POSSIBLE.
THIS GIRL IS INJURED. IT COSTS HER STRENGTH ...
...TO HEAL THAT WOUND...
BUT SHE'S PROTECT-ING HIM...
...AND FOCUS-ING HER ANGER ON ME.

THESE TWO MAY BE DIFFERENT.
WHAK

I'M SORRY I HAD TO LEAVE YOU, TANJIRO.
TAKE CARE OF NEZUKO.
SKFFF

HFF
HFF
HFF

HWSH
YOU'RE AWAKE?
HMMPH
TELL HIM THAT GIYU TOMIOKA SENT YOU.
GO SEE AN OLD MAN NAMED SAKONJI UROKODAKI WHO LIVES AT THE FOOT OF MOUNT SAGIRI.
WHSH
...BUT DON'T LET HER INTO DIRECT SUN-LIGHT.
YOUR SISTER SHOULD BE FINE BECAUSE THE SUN ISN'T OUT TODAY...

...

STARE

LET'S GO.

PRODUCTION ART, ILLUSTRATION ①

CHAPTER 2: THE STRANGER

I BEG YOUR PARDON...
...BUT MAY I TAKE THAT BASKET...
...AND A LITTLE STRAW AND BAMBOO?

WE DON'T MIND...
...BUT THE BASKET HAS A HOLE IN IT.
THAT'S ALL RIGHT. CAN I PAY YOU?
NO NEED. IT'S A BROKEN BASKET.

WE DON'T WANT IT!
BUT I *WANT* TO PAY!
WHAT A STUBBORN KID!

PLEASE LET ME PAY.
SHAKE SHAKE
NO, THANK YOU.
YOU CAN HAVE THE OTHER STUFF TOO.

SMACK
JUST TAKE IT! IT'S ONLY A FEW COINS ANYWAY!
OWWW!
THANK YOU VERY MUCH!
SHE'S GONE!
HMM?
NEZUKO...
NEZUKO!

...

POP
THERE SHE IS!

JUST WAIT.

SHE MUST REALLY NOT WANT THE SUNLIGHT TO HIT HER.
HER FACE IS SCRUNCHED UP.

MY SISTER IS LIKE A MOLE NOW.
DID SHE DIG THAT HOLE?

TA-DAH!

FWIK
FWIK
FWIK

...
GET IN.
HERE.
THE BASKET.
I WANT US TO TRAVEL DURING THE DAY.
I'LL CARRY YOU.
WILL YOU FIT IN HERE?

NEZUKO HAS GROWN UP.
I STILL THINK SHE'S A LITTLE GIRL.

YOU'RE TOO BIG.

...RE-VERSE THAT...
...AND GET SMALLER?
NEZUKO ...
...YOU'RE AS BIG AS AN ADULT. CAN YOU...

HMM?

STUFF
AH!
GET SMALL-ER!
NEZUKO.
SMALLER.
FLOP
FLOP
FWUP
YEOW!
OH! GOOD!

KAW
KAW
PAT PAT
THAT'S PERFECT!
GOOD GIRL, NEZUKO!
I'M IMPRESSED!
THE SUN WILL SET SOON.
TO GET TO MOUNT SAGIRI, YOU FIRST HAVE TO CROSS THAT MOUNTAIN.
AND YOU'RE GOING TO CARRY THAT HUGE LOAD? IT'S DANGER-OUS.
...SO DON'T GET LOST!
PEOPLE REALLY DO DISAPPEAR UP THERE...
BOW
THANK YOU VERY MUCH.
I'LL BE PLENTY CAREFUL.

OH!

!!
I SMELL BLOOD!

THERE'S A WAY STATION.
THERE'S A LIGHT ON. SOMEONE MUST BE THERE.
LET'S GO.

ARE YOU ALL RIGHT?
KLAK
KT
K

THESE MOUNTAIN PATHS ARE DANGER-OUS. THAT TRAVELER MAY BE INJURED!

WHAT?!
HEY!
THIS...
...IS MY TERRITORY!
GET AWAY FROM MY FEEDING GROUND!

...
HMM...?
SOMETHING'S WRONG HERE.
PLIP PLIP
A MAN-EATING DEMON!
ARE YOU TWO HUMAN?

WHIP
NH
OK

HA! HA!
NOT BAD!
A HATCHET ?!
HA!
FWMP
SEE?
THE BLEEDING ALREADY STOPPED!
BUT A WOUND LIKE THIS...
...WILL HEAL IN NO TIME!
VWP
ZWP.
ZWP
?!

HRF
HRF
HRF
HRF
HRF
FWAM
I'M GONNA SNAP YOUR NECK.
YOU'LL NEVER DO THAT AGAIN!
AND IN-CREDIBLY STRONG!
KRK
KRK
HE'S FAST!

WHOA

HRF
HRF
SH-SHE JUST KILLED HIM! WELL, HE WAS A DEMON, SO...

KO
NK

FWSH
N...
NEZUKO!
WHOK
THWIMP
!

WHY YOUUU ...!

I CAN'T BELIEVE IT! IT JUST MOVED WITH ITS HEAD RIPPED OFF!

WHAT ARE A DEMON AND A HUMAN DOING TOGETHER?!
I KNEW IT! ONE OF YOU IS A DEMON!
SOMETHING DIDN'T SEEM RIGHT!

TMP TMP TMP

IT'S STILL TALK-ING!!

GRRRP
!!
STOP!

SH
KCHA
K
YANK

GET OFF OF ME!
WHAT THE—? THE HEAD GREW ARMS?!
UR
GH
BO
NK

GRA
HH
GR
-P
THIS GUY'S TOUGH!
BIO
HIS HEAD...
N
K
...IS HARD!
TH
WP
PA
NG

CHOKE
MY HAIR IS TANGLED UP ON THE HAFT! AND I GREW THESE HANDS TOO SHORT, SO I CAN'T GET A GRIP!
ARGH!
HE PINNED ME TO THE TREE WITH HIS HATCHET!
NEZUKO!
WHSH

STOMP
THUD
KNOCK IT OFF!
ARGH!

GYAAAH!
SPLAT

HOW MANY DEMONS ARE THERE?
WOW!
SHNG

SO I HAVE TO DO THIS.
HFF
HFF
BUT...
...IF I DON'T KILL HIM, HE'LL ATTACK MORE PEOPLE.
HFF
HFF

A DIFFERENT DEMON.
HE SMELLS DIFFERENT THAN THE ONE THAT WAS AT MY HOUSE.

DO IT!

SK
FF
YOU CAN'T KILL IT WITH THAT.

PRODUCTION ART, ILLUSTRATION ②

CHAPTER 3: RETURN BY DAWN

GREETINGS ...
...LORD SAKONJI UROKODAKI.

I HAVE SENT A BOY YOUR WAY WHO SAYS HE WANTS TO BECOME A DEMON-SLAYING SWORDSMAN.

HE HAD THE COURAGE TO FIGHT ME UNARMED.
A DEMON SLAUGHTERED HIS FAMILY...

...TRANSFORMING HIS SURVIVING SISTER INTO A DEMON...
...BUT SHE CHOOSES NOT TO ATTACK HUMANS.

I BELIEVE THAT PERHAPS ...
LIKE YOU, THE BOY HAS A STRONG SENSE OF SMELL.
I SENSE SOMETHING IN THESE TWO THAT IS DIFFERENT FROM THE OTHERS.
I KNOW THIS IS A SELFISH REQUEST, SO PLEASE FORGIVE ME.
...HE COULD BE WORTHY OF CARRYING ON YOUR TRADITIONS.
PLEASE, TRAIN HIM.

MAY THIS FIND YOU IN GOOD HEALTH...
...AND IN GOOD SPIRITS.
SIN-CERELY ...
...GIYU TOMIOKA.

DON'T TRUST WHAT OTHERS SAY.
CAN'T YOU SOLVE THIS RIDDLE YOURSELF?
HE MOVED IN COMPLETE SILENCE.

H...
HOW CAN I FINISH IT OFF?
A TENGU MASK!

I'LL HAVE TO CRUSH THE HEAD...
...
NN GH
IF STABBING IT WON'T WORK...
ISN'T THERE ANY WAY TO KILL IT WITH ONE BLOW?
TO COMPLETELY CRUSH THE HEAD, I'LL HAVE TO SMASH IT WITH A ROCK REPEATEDLY.
IT WILL SURELY SUFFER.
SNIFF

WHEN FACING A DEMON, HE STILL REEKS OF SYMPATHY AND CONSIDERATION.
HE EVEN FEELS SYMPATHY FOR A DEMON.

HIS KINDNESS PREVENTS HIM FROM TAKING DECISIVE ACTION.

DAMN ...
...THIS KID IS NO GOOD.

I WAS UNCONSCIOUS.
I FEEL SICK.
IS MY BODY DEAD?

GIYU...
...THIS BOY IS USELESS.

WHA—?

WHILE I WAS WASTING TIME, THE MORNING HAS COME!
OH!
!!
WAH
GYAAH!
GYAAH!
GYAAH!
FLOP
FLOP
FLOP
SZZL
KRAKL

...

OH, YEAH...
...THAT GUY.

JUST A TOUCH OF SUN-LIGHT DID THAT?!
NO WONDER NEZUKO FEARS IT!

UM...

HE'S BURYING THE DEMON'S VICTIMS.

I AM SAKONJI UROKODAKI.
YOU MUST BE THE ONE GIYU TOLD ME ABOUT.
Y...
YES.
I'M TANJIRO KAMADO.
MY SISTER IS NEZUKO.
TELL ME, TANJIRO...
...WHAT WILL YOU DO WHEN YOUR SISTER EATS SOMEONE?

!!
YOU THINK TOO SLOWLY!

WHY COULDN'T YOU ANSWER THAT QUESTION IMMEDIATELY?
YOU ARE TOO SOFT!
...
YOU COULD NEVER FINISH OFF A DEMON BEFORE THE MORNING LIGHT.
YOU STRUGGLE OVER THE SIMPLEST DECISIONS.
THAT IS WHAT IT MEANS TO TRAVEL WITH YOUR SISTER WHO HAS BECOME A DEMON!
WHEN YOUR SISTER EATS SOMEONE, THERE ARE TWO THINGS YOU HAVE TO DO...
KILL YOUR SISTER... THEN SLIT YOUR OWN BELLY AND DIE!
DO YOU UNDER-STAND WHAT I AM SAYING?
YOUR SISTER MUST NEVER TAKE THE LIFE...
...OF AN INNOCENT PERSON!
BUT IT IS YOUR SACRED DUTY TO ENSURE THAT THIS NEVER HAPPENS.

VERY WELL...
...I WILL TEST YOU TO SEE IF YOU HAVE WHAT IT TAKES...
...TO BE A DEMON-SLAYER SWORDS-MAN.
YES!

SHOULDER YOUR SISTER AND FOLLOW ME.

HE'S FAST!
HFF
HF
HOW OLD IS THIS GUY?!
AND HIS FEET REALLY DON'T MAKE ANY SOUND!
HFF

BUT THEN...
... SUFFERING IS ALL YOU'VE EVER KNOWN...
...LITTLE SISTER.

NEZUKO...
...THIS'LL BE ROUGH, BUT HANG IN THERE!

EVERYTHING I COULDN'T GIVE TO THEM, I'LL GIVE TO YOU!

THE TEST BEGINS NOW.
CLIMB THE MOUN-TAIN.
WHEEZ
HFF
S...
WHEEZ
...DID I...
HFF
SO...
...PASS THE TEST?
FWIP
HFF
HFF
I'M DIZZY...
I'M ALREADY TIRED. MY LEGS ARE GETTING WEAK.
HFF
HFF

THIS TIME, I WILL NOT WAIT UNTIL SUNRISE.
NOW YOU MUST DESCEND TO THE HOUSE AT THE FOOT OF THE MOUNTAIN.

HFF
HFF
OH, I GET IT.
HE THINKS I'LL GET LOST IN THIS THICK FOG.

IS THAT ALL?
HFF
HFF

HUH?

I'VE ALREADY MEMORIZED UROKODAKI'S SCENT.
HFF
THAT'S EASY! I HAVE A SHARP NOSE!
HFF
I JUST HAVE TO GET BACK BEFORE SUNRISE.
HFF

SNAG
WHSH
EVEN IF I CAN'T SEE HIM, I CAN STILL FOLLOW HIM ALL THE WAY.
FOOM
FOOM
?!
WHAP
WHAP
WHAP

WHO'S THROWING ROCKS?!
FLMP
WHMP

I GET IT!
A COVERED PIT!
WSH
UH-OH! HERE WE GO AGAIN!
THESE ARE ALL TRAPS.
THAT'S THE CHALLENGE!
MMPH

THWOK

I'M IN BIG TROUBLE.
HFF
HFF

WHUD

AND I JUST NOTICED... UP ON THIS MOUNTAIN...
IF I KEEP SETTING OFF EVERY TRAP, I WON'T GET DOWN THE MOUNTAIN BY MORNING.

HFF
HFF
HFF
IT'S MUCH WORSE THAN THE MOUNTAIN WE LIVED ON!
...THE AIR'S SO THIN I CAN BARELY BREATHE!
HFF
HFF
CONTROL YOUR BREATHING. SNIFF OUT THE TRAPS.
I FEEL LIKE I MIGHT PASS OUT!
NO! I'VE GOTTA GET BACK!
THAT'S WHY I FEEL SO TIRED AND DIZZY.
YES! I CAN SMELL THEM!
TRAPS HAVE TO BE SET BY SOMEONE, AND THOSE SCENTS MUST LINGER.

BUT KNOWING THEY'RE THERE DOESN'T GRANT ME...
...THE ABILITY TO EVADE THEM ALL!

ZZZ
ZZZ
ZZZ

THUNK
KTK
THUNK

SHMP
SHMP
I...
...MADE IT...
...BACK.
HFF
HFF
HFF
...I ACCEPT YOU AS MY STUDENT!
TANJIRO KAMADO...

- 鬼滅奇譚 (Kimetsu Kitan) (Mysterious Story of the Demon Slayer)
- 鬼鬼滅滅 (Kikimetsumetsu) (Demon Demon Slayer Slayer)
- 悪鬼滅々 (Akkimetsumetsu) (Evil Demon Slayer)
- 鬼殺の刃 (Kisatsu no Yaiba) (Sword of the Demon Killer)
- 滅々鬼譚 (Metsumetsu Kitan) (Strange Tale of the Demon Slayer)
- 鬼殺譚 (Kisatsutan) (Tale of the Demon Killer)
- 空想鬼滅奇譚 (Kuso Kimetsu Kitan) (The Fantastic Strange Tale of the Demon Slayer)
- 鬼狩りカグツチ (Onigari Kagutsuchi) (Demon Hunting God of Fire)
- 炭のカグツチ (Sumi no Kagutsuchi) (Charred God of Fire)

CHAPTER 4: TANJIRO'S JOURNAL, PART 1

THERE ARE A FEW HUNDRED MEMBERS ...
...OF THE DEMON SLAYER CORPS.
THE ORGANIZATION ISN'T OFFICIALLY RECOGNIZED BY THE GOVERNMENT.
BUT IT HAS EXISTED SINCE DAYS OF OLD AND STILL HUNTS DEMONS TODAY.
HOWEVER, THE IDENTITY OF THE LEADER OF THE DEMON SLAYER CORPS...
...IS SHROUDED IN MYSTERY.

DEMON
THEY HAVE IMPRESSIVE PHYSICAL ABILITIES AND THEIR WOUNDS HEAL QUICKLY.
STAPLE FOOD: HUMANS.
THEY CAN RECONNECT SEVERED FLESH AND GROW NEW LIMBS. SOME DEMONS CAN CHANGE FORM. OTHERS POSSESS STRANGE POWERS.
THEY KILL HUMANS AND EAT THEM.
IT IS UNCLEAR WHEN OR WHERE THEY FIRST APPEARED.
THE ONLY WAYS TO KILL THEM ARE BY EXPOSING THEM TO SUNLIGHT OR BY CUTTING OFF THEIR HEADS WITH A SPECIAL SWORD.

THEY ARE HUMAN, SO THEIR WOUNDS HEAL SLOWLY AND LOST LIMBS DO NOT RETURN.
THE DEMON SLAYER CORPS FIGHTS DEMONS FACE-TO-FACE.
NONETHE-LESS, THEY FIGHT DEMONS IN ORDER TO PROTECT ORDINARY PEOPLE.

THERE ARE MANY TRAINERS. IN DIFFERENT PLACES, THEY USE VARIOUS TRAINING METHODS.
I AM A TRAINER.
JUST LIKE IT SOUNDS, I TRAIN SWORDS-MEN.

I DECIDE WHETHER YOU MAY ATTEMPT FINAL SELECTION.
IN ORDER TO JOIN THE DEMON SLAYER CORPS, YOU MUST SURVIVE THE FINAL SELECTION AT MOUNT FUJIKASANE.

STARTING TODAY, I HAVE DECIDED TO WRITE THIS JOURNAL FOR NEZUKO.
AGAIN TODAY, I DESCENDED THE MOUNTAIN.
I TRAIN AS HARD AS I CAN SO I WON'T DIE DURING FINAL SELECTION.
I GO DOWN THE MOUNTAIN REPEATEDLY, DAY AFTER DAY. I'VE BECOME QUITE GOOD AT AVOIDING TRAPS.
I'M GROWING STRONGER ...
...AND MY NOSE IS EVEN SHARPER AT PICKING UP SCENTS.

IT'S LIKE HE REALLY WANTS TO KILL ME.
THOK THOK
BUT THE TRAPS ARE GETTING MUCH DEADLIER.
IT REALLY GETS IN THE WAY...
...SO CARRYING IT GOT ME CAUGHT IN A LOT OF TRAPS.
TODAY, I WENT DOWN THE MOUNTAIN WITH A KATANA.
AFTER DESCENDING THE MOUNTAIN, I SWING THE SWORD SO MUCH I FEEL LIKE MY ARMS MIGHT FALL OFF.
SWSH
SWSH
...715...
...716...
I SAY "TODAY," BUT LATELY I DO THIS EVERY DAY.
TODAY, I PRACTICED SWINGING THE SWORD.
...713...
...714...

WITH A KATANA ...
IT'S STRONG AGAINST FORCE LENGTHWISE BUT WEAK AGAINST FORCE FROM THE SIDE.
THE FIRST THING HE TAUGHT ME WAS THAT A KATANA BREAKS EASILY.
WHEN YOU SWING A KATANA...
...YOU MUST ATTACK STRAIGHT AHEAD.
...THE DIRECTION OF THE BLADE AND THE DIRECTION OF THE FORCE YOU APPLY MUST BE EXACTLY THE SAME.
...HE'LL BREAK MY BONES. HIS THREATS ARE COLD...
IN OTHER WORDS, IF I BREAK IT...
FURTHER-MORE...
...YOU!
...IF YOU DAMAGE THE SWORD, HE'LL DAMAGE...
...LIKE THE MOUNTAIN.

TODAY, I DID NOTHING BUT FALL DOWN...
...TRAINING TO BREAK MY FALL AND GET UP QUICKLY.
URO-KODAKI STANDS AGAINST ME...
...UN-ARMED.
I WIELD MY SWORD AND FACE UROKODAKI WITH THE INTENT TO STRIKE HIM DOWN.

HE EASILY THROWS ME TO THE GROUND.
FWSH
HUUUH?!
BUT HE'S RIDICU-LOUSLY STRONG.
I'VE BEEN WRIT-ING...
...FOR SIX MONTHS, NEZUKO, AND YOU STILL HAVEN'T WOKEN UP.
TODAY, I LEARNED BREATHING AND SOME STANDARD FORMS.
LIKE THIS?
NO!
THIS?
NO!
THIS?
NO!
HE SAID I DIDN'T HAVE ENOUGH STRENGTH IN MY CORE, THEN HE GOT ANGRY AND HIT MY STOMACH.
BAM
AAGH!
BAM

YET IT'S CLEARLY STRANGE FOR YOU TO KEEP SLEEPING LIKE THIS.
UROKODAKI IMMEDIATELY CALLED A DOCTOR TO LOOK AT YOU...
...BUT HE FOUND NOTHING WRONG.
AND ...
I THOUGHT I'D WAKE UP IN THE MORNING TO FIND YOU DEAD.
I WAS SCARED.
...THAT'S STILL HOW I FEEL EVERY NIGHT.
MANY TIMES I'VE THOUGHT THAT I WOULD DIE.
AND EVERY DAY I GO HIGHER ON THE MOUNTAIN FOR MY TRAINING, EACH PLACE MORE DANGEROUS AND WITH THINNER AIR.

I HAVE NOTHING MORE TO TEACH YOU.

HUH?
HFF
HZZ
HZZ
ABOUT A YEAR AFTER I ARRIVED AT MOUNT SAGIRI...
...THAT WAS ALL HE SAID.

THE REST IS UP TO YOU.
CAN YOU...
...TAKE WHAT I HAVE TAUGHT YOU AND BRING IT TO THE NEXT LEVEL?

IF YOU CAN SPLIT THIS BOULDER, I WILL APPROVE YOU FOR FINAL SELECTION.

CAN YOU SPLIT IT WITH A KATANA?
CAN THAT EVEN BE SPLIT?!
A BOULDER ...?
THE BLADE WOULD BREAK.
I DON'T THINK I CAN.
UROKO-DAKI!!
UROKO-DAKI!
WAIT! THIS...
STOMP
...HASN'T TAUGHT ME ANYTHING.
... UROKO-DAKI ...
SINCE THAT DAY...

SWSH SWSH SWSH
HOLDING MY BREATH, FLEXIBILITY, AND THE MOST BASIC THINGS TOO.
STILL...
...EVERY DAY I PRACTICE WHAT I LEARNED FROM UROKO-DAKI.
I'M GLAD I WROTE EVERYTHING DOWN IN MY JOURNAL.

I'M BEGIN-NING TO WORRY.
BUT EVEN AFTER HALF A YEAR I STILL CAN'T SPLIT THE BOULDER.

I HAVE TO DO MORE.
MORE!
I HAVEN'T HAD ENOUGH TRAINING.
IT ISN'T ENOUGH.

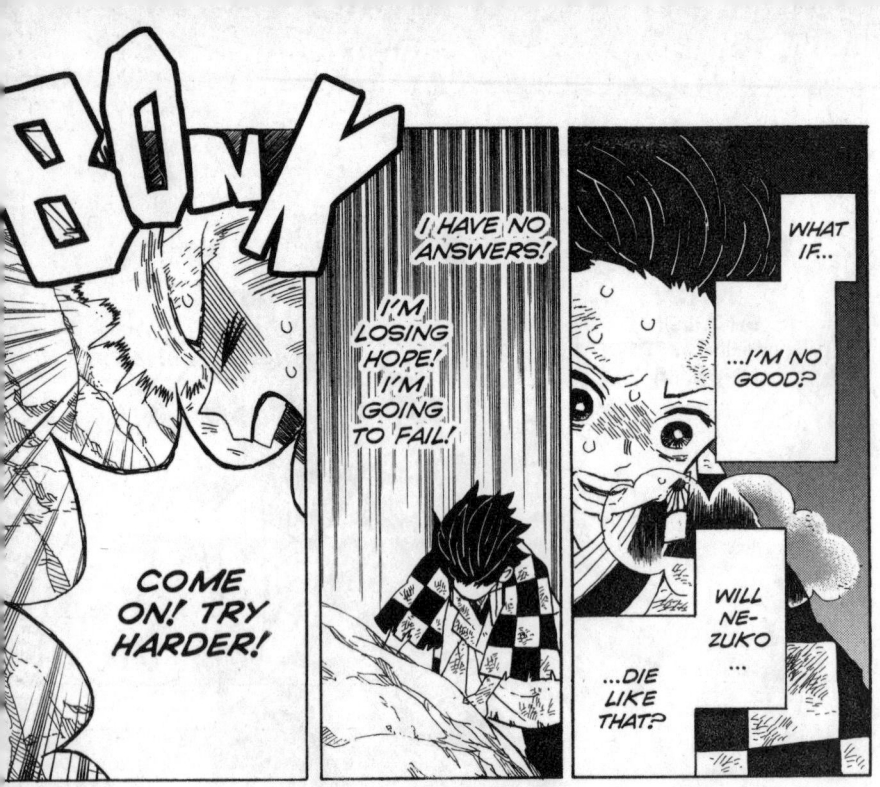
BONK
COME ON! TRY HARDER!
I HAVE NO ANSWERS!
I'M LOSING HOPE! I'M GOING TO FAIL!
WHAT IF...
...I'M NO GOOD?
WILL NE-ZUKO ...
...DIE LIKE THAT?

SILENCE!

A MAN SHOULDN'T WHINE... IT'S UNSEEMLY.

I CAN'T SMELL HIM!
A FOX MASK...?
WHERE DID HE COME FROM?!
?!

FWSH

!!

WHATEVER THE SUFFERING, BEAR IT IN SILENCE.
IF YOU'RE A MAN.
OR ARE YOU STILL A LITTLE BOY?

WHAK
THUD
BOOF
UGH!

YOU'RE SLOW...
...AND WEAK...
...AND IMMATURE.
YOU'LL NEVER BE A DEMON SLAYER.

ADVERTISING ILLUSTRATION AT THE BEGINNING OF THE SERIES.

CHAPTER 5: TANJIRO'S JOURNAL, PART 2

WHAT ARE YOU DOING?
WHERE'D YOU COME FROM?!

!!

HOW LONG DO YOU PLAN TO HAVE YOUR BUTT STUCK IN THE MUD?
TAKE A STANCE!

DOING?
I'M TRAIN-ING.

NOW... ATTACK!
STOMP
BUT...
...YOU HAVE A WOODEN SWORD AND I HAVE A REAL ONE!
HA HA!
HA HA HA HA!
HA HA HA HA!

HA HA HA HA!
...
HA HA HA!
WA HA HA HA!

WHAK
KLAK
YOU THINK YOU CAN HURT ME?
THANKS FOR WORRYING ABOUT ME!
HOW SWEET!

YOU CAN'T HURT ME! I'M STRONGER THAN YOU'LL EVER BE! I'VE ALREADY SPLIT A BOULDER!
WP
REST YOUR POOR, SOFT HEART.

FWAM
YOU'VE GAINED NOTHING. YOU HAVEN'T MASTERED ANYTHING!

YOU SPLIT A BOULDER ?!

YOU JUST MEMORIZED IT AS A FACT...
BUT YOUR BODY DOESN'T UNDER-STAND ANYTHING!

CER-TAINLY NOT...
...THE BREATHING TECHNIQUE TAUGHT BY UROKODAKI!
TOTAL CONCEN-TRATION BREATHING!

HE KNOWS UROKODAKI?! AND ABOUT THE BREATHING...
!!

BEAT IT INTO THE MARROW OF YOUR BONES!
I DO!
AS HARD AS I CAN!
I DO, EVERY DAY!
BUT NO MATTER HOW HARD I TRY...
I CAN'T PROG-RESS ANY FURTHER.
WHACK
WHAM
BEAT IT INTO YOUR FLESH AND BLOOD!
MORE!
MORE!
WHAP
MORE!
SO THAT YOU BECOME THE EMBODIMENT OF THE SECRETS UROKODAKI TAUGHT YOU!
WHAM

...IS TO LIE DOWN AND DIE! SO MAKE YOURSELF PROGRESS!
DON'T "TRY"... JUST DO IT!
IF YOU'RE A MAN!
THE ONLY OTHER CHOICE...
SHOW ME...
...YOUR STRENGTH!
ATTACK! WHAT HAVE YOU GOT?
AAAAAGH!!

KRAK

THUD
HMM.
FWP
I LEAVE THE REST TO YOU.

ARE YOU ALL RIGHT?
DID YOU SEE WHAT HAPPENED?
?
SH
WF

THAT'S HOW I WANT TO BE TOO!
BUT IS THAT EVEN POS-SIBLE?
CAN I DO IT...?
THAT WAS AN INCREDIBLE BLOW!
NOT A BIT OF UNNECES-SARY MOTION!
IT WAS TRULY BEAUTIFUL!
UH... WHO ARE YOU?
SHE'S CUTE...
I'M SURE YOU CAN.
I'LL WATCH OVER YOU.
...AND TELLS ME THE GUY'S NAME IS SABITO.
SHE SAYS HER NAME IS MAKOMO...

SHE CORRECTS MY UNNECESSARY MOVEMENTS AND BAD HABITS.
MAKOMO POINTS OUT THE DEFECTS IN MY STYLE.

I ASK, BUT SHE NEVER TELLS ME.
WHERE DID SHE COME FROM?
WHY IS SHE DOING THIS FOR ME?

SHE OFTEN SAYS THOSE WORDS.
WE REALLY LIKE URO-KODAKI.

THERE ARE OTHER CHILDREN TOO.
THEY'RE ALL AROUND, WATCHING YOU.

THEY AREN'T SIBLINGS. THEY WERE BOTH ORPHANS.
UROKO-DAKI TOOK THEM IN AND RAISED THEM.

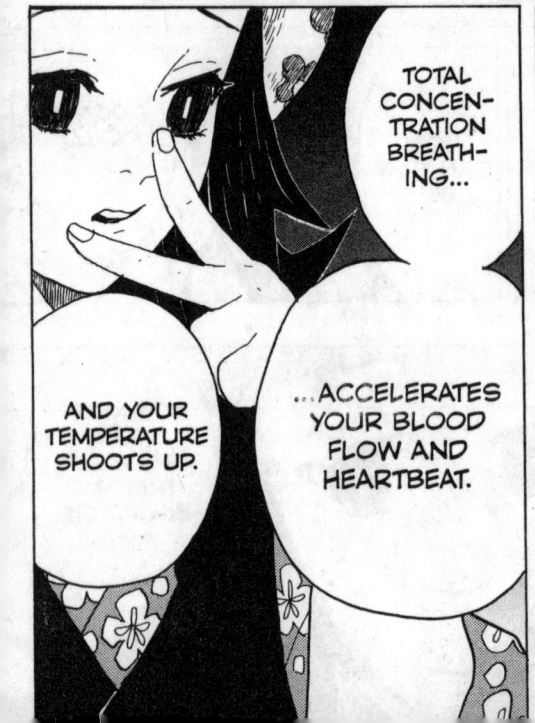
TOTAL CONCEN-TRATION BREATH-ING...
...ACCELERATES YOUR BLOOD FLOW AND HEARTBEAT.
AND YOUR TEMPERATURE SHOOTS UP.

MAKOMO IS A BIT OF A STRANGE GIRL.
SHE SAYS THINGS IN A WEIRD WAY.
?
?

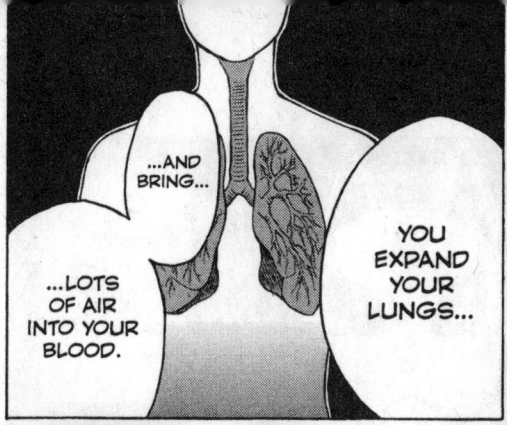
YOU EXPAND YOUR LUNGS...
...AND BRING...
...LOTS OF AIR INTO YOUR BLOOD.

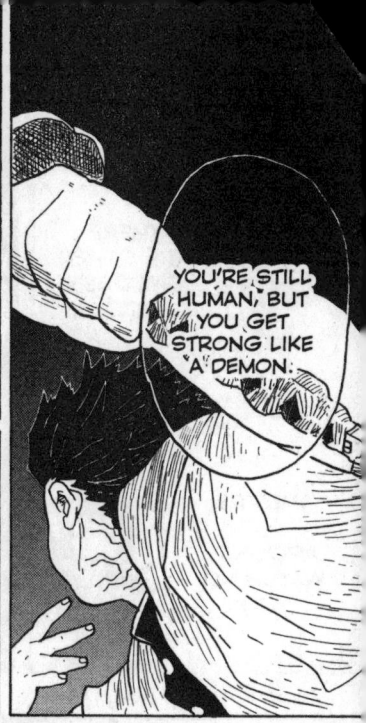
YOU'RE STILL HUMAN, BUT YOU GET STRONG LIKE A DEMON.

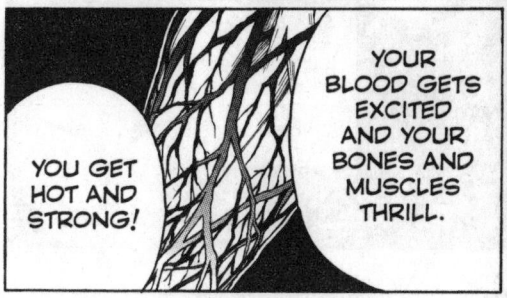
YOUR BLOOD GETS EXCITED AND YOUR BONES AND MUSCLES THRILL.
YOU GET HOT AND STRONG!

I DON'T REALLY GET IT...
HOW CAN THAT BE?

YOU MUST TRAIN SO HARD THAT YOU COULD DIE.
BASICALLY, I DON'T THINK THERE'S ANY-THING ELSE YOU CAN DO.

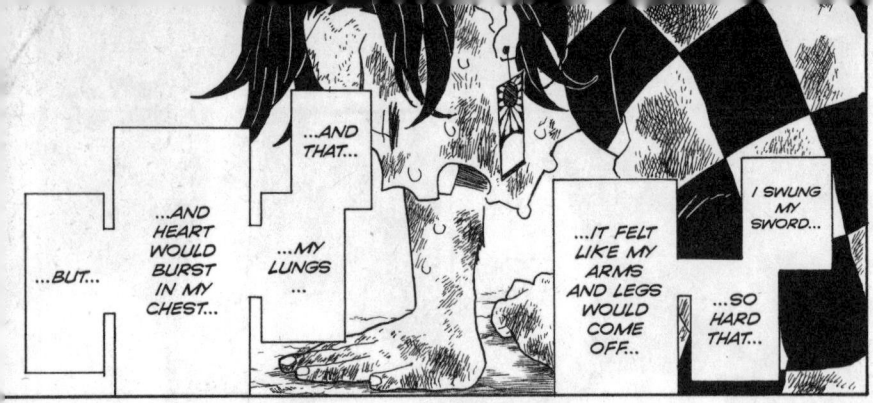
I SWUNG MY SWORD...
...SO HARD THAT...
...IT FELT LIKE MY ARMS AND LEGS WOULD COME OFF...
...AND THAT...
...MY LUNGS ...
...AND HEART WOULD BURST IN MY CHEST...
...BUT...

...I STILL COULDN'T BEAT SABITO.

...WHEN I WENT TO FACE SABITO...
...HE HELD A REAL SWORD.

ANOTHER SIX MONTHS PASSED. UNTIL ONE DAY...

TODAY, I WILL WIN.
THE CONTEST WAS SIMPLE.
THE STRONGER, FASTER BLADE WINS.
AFTER HALF A YEAR...
...YOU'VE FINALLY GOT THE FACE OF A MAN.

THE FIGHT WAS OVER IN AN INSTANT.
THAT DAY, IN THAT MOMENT, FOR THE FIRST TIME...
...MY BLADE REACHED SABITO FIRST.
GASP

WHEN I WON, SABITO SMILED.
IT SEEMED LIKE A SAD SMILE TO ME...
...OR MAYBE PROUD AND REASSURING.
WIN, TANJIRO...
...AGAINST THEM TOO.
FWSH
SUDDENLY, SABITO DISAPPEARED...

...AND I FOUND THAT MY SWORD HAD NOT CUT SABITO'S MASK.
IT HAD SPLIT THE BOULDER.

WORDS OF GRATITUDE

Thank you to everyone who read this work and to everyone who bought it. Thanks to your support, the series will continue. I can't tell you how thankful I am. Unlike water and food, manga isn't absolutely necessary for survival. Getting you to buy it is a tough job. Thank you very much. I create this manga with the help of many people. I'll work even harder to keep it interesting for you, so please keep reading. And again... thank you!!

CHAPTER 6: A MOUNTAIN OF HANDS

WHEN I'M FIGHTING SOME-ONE...
...AND I FIND THAT SCENT, I SEE THE THREAD.
THANKS TO MY TRAINING WITH MAKOMO ...
...I'VE LEARNED TO SMELL OUT AN "OPENING THREAD." THAT'S HOW I WON.
GUIDED BY THE THREAD, MY BLADE CUTS INTO THAT SPOT.
IT RUNS FROM MY BLADE...
...TO A SPOT ON MY OPPONENT, AND IT GOES TAUT THE MOMENT I SEE IT.

I HAD NO WISH TO SEE ANOTHER CHILD DIE.
I DIDN'T THINK YOU WOULD SPLIT THAT BOULDER...
I DID NOT INTEND TO SEND YOU TO FINAL SELECTION.

...BUT YOU DID WELL.

TANJIRO ...
...YOU...
...ARE AN AMAZING CHILD.

GO TO FINAL SELEC-TION...
...BUT BE SURE TO RETURN ALIVE.
YOUR SISTER AND I ARE HERE WAITING.

AFTER CUTTING MY HAIR...
UROKODAKI GAVE ME A MASK.
IT'S CALLED A WARDING MASK.
APPARENTLY, IT OFFERS PROTECTION FROM EVIL.

I CAN'T TAKE NEZUKO WITH ME—SHE'S STILL ASLEEP.
SO I'M LEAVING HER IN UROKO-DAKI'S CARE.

I'M ON MY WAY, UROKODAKI!
GIVE MY BEST TO SABITO AND MAKOMO!
TANJIRO ...
...HOW IS IT YOU...
...KNOW THE NAMES OF THOSE DECEASED CHILDREN?

MOUNT FUJIKASANE: SITE OF FINAL SELECTION
WOW!
BUT WISTERIA ...
... SHOULDN'T BE BLOOMING THIS TIME OF YEAR.

LOOK HOW MANY THERE ARE!

GREETINGS, EVERYONE.
THANK YOU FOR GATHERING TONIGHT FOR FINAL SELECTION.
MOUNT FUJIKASANE HOLDS DEMONS THAT DEMON-SLAYER SWORDSMEN HAVE TAKEN ALIVE AND TRAPPED HERE.
DEMONS HATE WISTERIA FLOWERS, WHICH BLOOM HERE EVEN OUT OF SEASON.
THEY COVER THE MOUNTAIN FROM ITS FOOT TO HALFWAY UP THE SLOPE.

IF YOU DO, THEN YOU WILL HAVE PASSED FINAL SELECTION.
NOW GO.
HOWEVER, FROM THAT POINT ON, THE WISTERIA DOES NOT BLOOM. SO THE DEMONS ROAM FREE.
YOU MUST SURVIVE THERE FOR SEVEN DAYS.
WHS
H

TWO OF THEM! OUT OF NOWHERE!
BUMP
NO, YOU GET LOST!
CAN I WIN?
BUMP
BUMP
HEY! HEY!
I'M GONNA EAT THIS KID!
GET LOST!
HE'S MY MEAL!
SHUT UP!

KKS
THE ONE WHO KILLS HIM FIRST GETS TO EAT HIM!
IT'S BEEN SO LONG SINCE I TASTED HUMAN FLESH!
WATER BREATHING!
FW
TOTAL CONCEN-TRATION ...

I SMELL THE THREAD!

FOURTH FORM:
STRIKING TIDE!

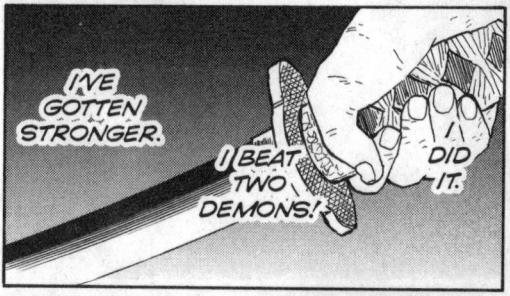
I'VE GOTTEN STRONGER.
I BEAT TWO DEMONS!
I DID IT.

...I CAN DO THIS!
ALL THAT TRAINING WORKED...

REST IN PEACE!

...EVEN THE BONES CRUMBLE!
WHEN I USE THE KATANA THAT URO-KODAKI GAVE ME...

KRA
RK
SH

WHAT'S THAT ROTTEN SMELL?
UGH!
SNIFF
WAAAH!
WHSH
THERE'S A HUGE, DEFORMED DEMON BACK THERE!
I'VE NEVER SEEN ANY-THING LIKE IT!
THMP

BLRB
BRBL
GYAAAH!
AN
K

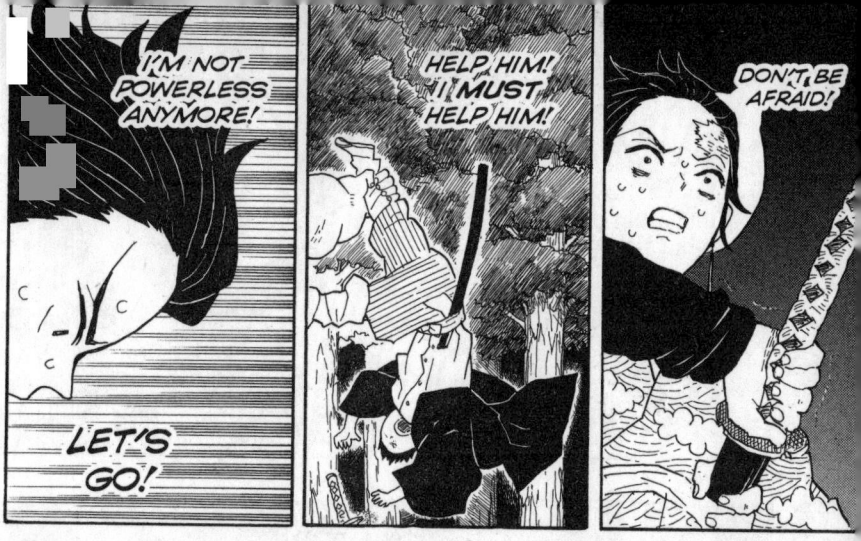

WATER BREATH-ING

SECOND FORM:

WATER WHEEL!

...FOXES HAS COME!
GLARE
ANOTHER OF MY DEAR...

TAISHO WHISPERS & RUMORS
I heard one of them is a boy...

CHAPTER 7: SPIRITS OF THE DECEASED

DO YOU THINK...
...TANJIRO CAN REALLY DO IT?

SABITO ...?

I DON'T KNOW.
BUT...
...NO AMOUNT OF EFFORT IS TOO MUCH.
AND YOU KNOW THAT...
...RIGHT?

THE IMPERIAL FAMILY IS TAISHO!
?!
...
SHIN
TELL ME, FOX BOY...
...RIGHT NOW...
...WHAT MEIJI EMPEROR SITS UPON THE THRONE?
GAAAAGH!
I'VE BEEN HERE SO LONG...
...THAT DYNASTIES HAVE RISEN AND FALLEN!

WOOOE
DAMN UROKO-DAKI!
DAMN UROKO-DAKI!
DAMN UROKO-DAKI!
DAMN HIM!
BRBL
BLRB

...
GAAAGH!
AGAIN AND AGAIN!
ALL WHILE I'VE BEEN TRAPPED HERE!
UNFOR-GIVABLE! UNFOR-GIVABLE!

IT'S BEEN 47 TORTUROUS YEARS!
OH, I KNOW HIM! UROKODAKI WAS THE ONE WHO CAPTURED ME! I WILL NEVER FORGET!

YOU KNOW URO—

IN THE EDO PERIOD... THE KEIO ERA!
BACK THEN HE WAS STILL A DEMON SLAYER!

NO DEMON HERE HAS BEEN ALIVE THAT LONG!
LIES!
YOU'RE LYING!
DEMON HUNTER... EDO PERIOD?!
...AND THEY GET KILLED DURING SELECTION!
PLUS, THE DEMONS EAT EACH OTHER TOO!
THEY ONLY PUT DEMONS UP HERE THAT HAVE EATEN TWO OR THREE PEOPLE...
...I HAVE EATEN 50 OF YOU BRATS!
BUT I HAVE SURVIVED A VERY LONG TIME. IN THIS PRISON...
...OF WISTERIA BLOSSOMS ...

...A DEMON'S STRENGTH COMES FROM THE NUMBER OF PEOPLE IT HAS CONSUMED.
REMEM-BER...
FIFTY?!

...AND SOME PHYSICALLY CHANGE, GAINING UNNATURAL POWERS.
THAT'S RIGHT. THEY GROW STRON-GER...

IF IT EATS MANY PEOPLE IT GETS STRONGER?

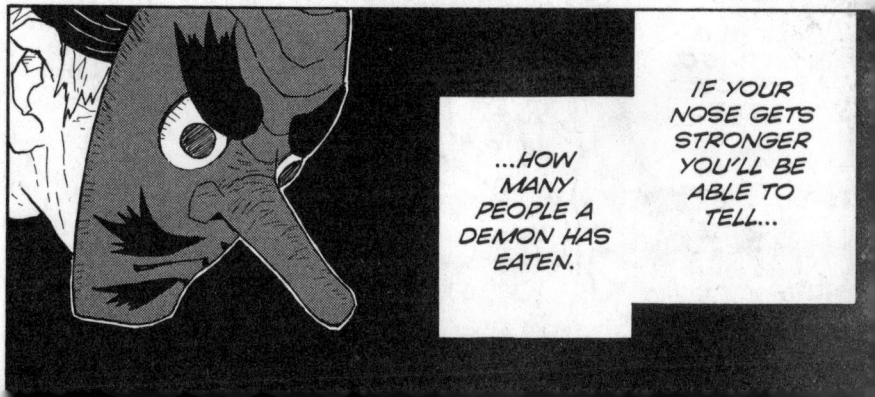
...HOW MANY PEOPLE A DEMON HAS EATEN.
IF YOUR NOSE GETS STRONGER YOU'LL BE ABLE TO TELL...

?!
WHAT ARE YOU TALKING ABOUT?
...12...
...YOU ARE NUMBER 14.
...13...
... AND ...
I'VE DECIDED TO KILL *ALL* OF HIS STUDENTS!
THAT'S HOW MANY OF *UROKODAKI'S STUDENTS* I HAVE EATEN!
HEE HEE
HEE
HEE
HEE

THE OTHER WAS A GIRL-BRAT WHOSE KIMONO WAS COVERED IN FLOWERS.
SHE WAS SMALL AND NOT SO STRONG...
...BUT SHE WAS VERY AGILE.
HE HAD A COLORFUL JACKET, AND WAS THE STRONGEST BY FAR.
HE HAD PEACH-COLORED HAIR AND A SCAR BY HIS MOUTH.
THIRTEEN OF URO-KADAKI'S STUDENTS, BUT ABOVE ALL...
YES, INDEED!
...TWO OF THEM...
...I'LL NEVER FORGET.

HOW COULD THIS DEMON HAVE KILLED THEM? THEY TRAINED ME!

I RECOGNIZE YOU...
...BY THOSE FOX MASKS.
I KNOW THE GRAIN OF THOSE MASKS THAT UROKO-DAKI CARVES.
THEY'RE CARVED THE SAME WAY AS THE TENGU MASK HE WORE.

HFF
THEY'RE ALL INSIDE MY STOMACH.
HFF
IT'S LIKE UROKODAKI FED THEM TO ME!
HFF

DID HE CALL IT A "WARDING MASK"?
I ATE THEM ALL *BECAUSE* OF THE MASKS THEY WORE.

HEH HEH...
HEH HEH HEH HEH...
THE GIRL-BRAT WEPT AND GREW ANGRY WHEN I TOLD HER THAT.
HEH HEH HEH HEH...

SOON HER MOVEMENTS GOT SHAKY.
HEH HEH HEH!
THEN I RIPPED OFF HER ARMS AND LEGS!

STAY CALM, TANJIRO.
YOUR BREATHING IS UNEVEN.
DON'T WORRY ABOUT US! FOCUS ON WHAT YOU MUST DO!
WHAM

WHILE IT'S BEATING ON HIM, I'LL RUN AWAY!
FLAM
WHSH
KRAK

WAKE UP, BIG BROTHER!
WHS
WHAM
BAM

A STRANGE SMELL FROM THE GROUND!
NO MATTER HOW MANY ARMS I CUT OFF, IT GROWS MORE!
HUH ?!

I MISSED! HE NOTICED MY HANDS UNDER-GROUND...
...AND LEAPT AWAY! AND WHAT A LEAP!
BUT IN MIDAIR...
DOWN
UP

...HE CAN'T DODGE THIS ATTACK!
GWAAH
WHONK

THE FOX-BRAT IS IN STRIKING RANGE!
I CAN'T GROW MORE IN TIME!
AND I'M OUT OF HANDS!
HE ESCAPED!
WATER BREATHING!
TOTAL CONCENTRA-TION.
EVEN THE PEACH-HAIR COULDN'T CUT IT!
BUT MY NECK IS HARD AND IMPERVI-OUS!
SNIFF
...AND CRUSH IT, JUST LIKE I DID TO THE OTHER ONE!
WHEN HE FAILS TO CUT MY NECK, I'LL GRAB HIS HEAD...

IS IT POSSIBLE THAT TANJIRO WILL LOSE TOO?
THAT THING'S NECK IS SO HARD.
HE MAY LOSE OR HE MAY WIN.
BUT ONE THING IS FOR CERTAIN...
PING

THE BOULDER THAT TANJIRO CUT WAS BIGGER AND HARDER THAN ANYONE HAD EVER CUT BEFORE!
HRAAAAAAH!!

VOLUME 1 — CRUELTY (THE END)

YOU'RE READING THE WRONG WAY!

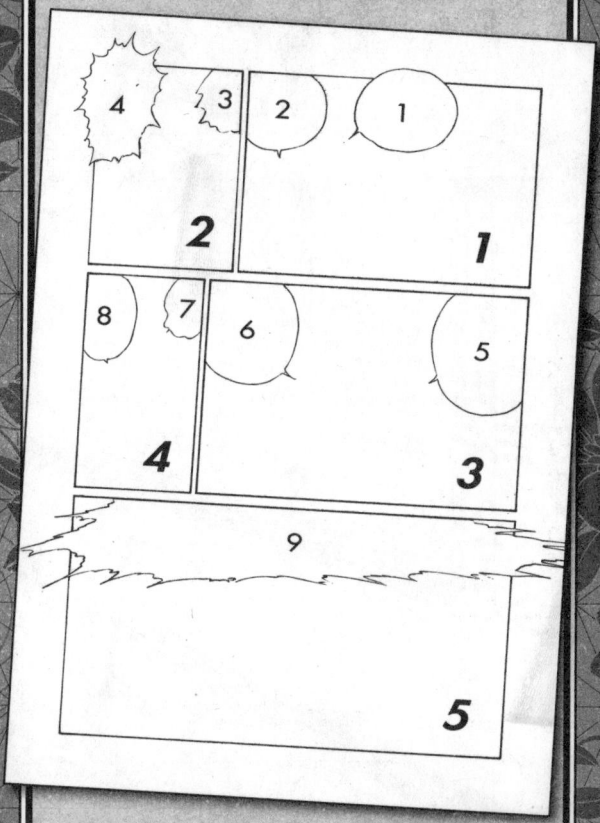

DEMON SLAYER: KIMETSU NO YAIBA reads from right to left, starting in the upper-right corner. Japanese is read from right to left, meaning that action, sound effects and word-balloon order are completely reversed from English order.

DEMON SLAYER

KIMETSU NO YAIBA

D0036576

In Taisho-era Japan, kindhearted Tanjiro Kamado makes a living selling charcoal. But his peaceful life is shattered when a demon slaughters his entire family. His little sister Nezuko is the only survivor, but she has been transformed into a demon herself! Tanjiro sets out on a dangerous journey to find a way to return his sister to normal and destroy the demon who ruined his life.

Learning to slay demons won't be easy, and Tanjiro barely knows where to start. The surprise appearance of another boy named Giyu, who seems to know what's going on, might provide some answers—but only if Tanjiro can stop Giyu from killing his sister first!

$9.99 USA $12.99 CAN £7.99 UK

viz.com

ISBN: 978-1-9747-0052-3

50999

9 781974 700523

VIZ MEDIA SHONEN JUMP RATED T TEEN